# Vegan on a Budget

## Making Veganism an Affordable Lifestyle

©2015

D1798817

Vegan on a Budget

Making Veganism an Affordable Lifestyle

June 22, 2015

Copyright ©2015 One Jacked Monkey, LLC

onejackedmonkey.com

ISBN-13: 978-1514665541

ISBN-10: 1514665549

Additional contributions by Emma Cogan

## Disclaimer

Although the author and publisher have made every effort to ensure that the information in this book was correct at press time, the author and publisher do not assume and hereby disclaim any liability to any party for any loss, damage, or disruption caused by errors or omissions, whether such errors or omissions result from negligence, accident, or any other cause.

# Grab the
# 10 Best
# Vegan Recipes
## That Are Cheap, Quick and Easy to
# Make...FREE!

"The 10 Best Vegan Dishes" has just what you need to satisfy your appetite, to spare your money and to save you time:

- ➢ 3 Awesome Varieties of Breakfast
- ➢ 4 Different Delicious Lunches
- ➢ 3 Distinct Dinner Dishes
- ➢ Many tips and notes to get the most out of every dish
- ➢ Options and alternatives for some recipes

Have you struggled with finding GOOD vegan recipes that are easy to make? Are you needing to find recipes that are tasty AND cheap?

With 10 vegan recipes and a number of options and alternatives to some of the dishes, you will have plenty of vibrant, flavorful meals that will fill you up, keep you healthy and looking forward to your next meal.

## ***Get this book FREE***

## Go to http://eepurl.com/bfE46z to

## get a free copy sent to your email

# Table of Contents

# Introduction: The True Cost of Food

Low prices seem to drive today's food industry. Sale signs and discounts line every aisle of all supermarkets. It is impossible to miss a buy one, get one free deal or buy one, get one half off advertisement. It's great news that food is becoming more affordable than it used to be. However, does it ever make you wonder how farmers and companies manage to sell food so cheaply and still make a profit? Is it all good news? When we think about our spending habits, do we ever think about the impact our habits have on the planet? Or do we just think about the cost to our wallets?

The average American spends just 7% of their total expenses on food. On one hand, this makes sense. The United States is a high-income country, and even its poorest citizens fare better than citizens in low-income countries. The United States spends far less on food than any other high-income countries. Even other high-income countries like France and Germany spend more money on food than the United States. For instance, the average French citizen spends nearly double that, 13.5% of their income on food. The average German citizen invests 11.4% of their earnings on groceries.[1]

It is a remarkable achievement that Americans can spend such a small amount of their incomes on food. Undernutrition, the type of malnutrition due to caloric deficit intake, is a rare find in the United States. The average reader looking at these reports does not realize that there is a high cost to these low prices. Michael Pollan, a renowned critic of the American food industry calls these costs "externalized costs." The cost of your $5.00 frozen bulk package of "Chicken Nuggets" is not just $5.00. That low cost stems from businesses using cruel livestock industry practices and paying workers low wages with few benefits. Cheap food can also have a negative impact on one's health. For instance, cheap food often has unhealthy ingredients that lead to rising obesity rates and chronic obesity-related illnesses.[2] For food companies to keep prices low and still make a profit, they have to sacrifice quality and ethics for their profit.

What's the solution? Do I need to shop at an expensive health food store or fastidiously research each product I purchase to make sure the food on my table is ethically and healthy? Is there any way someone with a limited budget can adhere to their morals and values when grocery shopping in America today?

Here is the solution: veganism. You don't need to spend a fortune on packaged vegan food and hard-to-find super foods. My answer is simple, traditional veganism, without marked-up kale chips and chia seed soy yogurt. However, if you want to eat kale chips, you can certainly make those yourself at a fraction of the cost for pre-made ones in the store. It all depends on your spending habits.

In regards to spending habits, how would you classify yourself? Are you someone who pays attention to the advertisements? Would you call yourself thrifty or do you take a more liberal viewpoint towards your spending? The answer, according to the United States Department of Agriculture (USDA), may surprise you. The USDA uses the following terms to categorize expenditures on food:

- Thrifty Plan
- Low-Cost Plan
- Moderate Cost Plan
- Liberal Plan

What would a thrifty, thirty-year-old female spend each week on food? Specifically, how much money do you think this person spends on groceries?

Does $50 sound realistic? In fact, she spends just $38.20. That $50-$60 guess aligns with the moderate plan. Someone who falls under this plan spends $59.80 on food per week. The results are nationwide, so the spending does not factor in higher costs of living in places like San Francisco, New York, or Washington D.C.[3]

When I read the spending plans for individuals and families, I wondered what are they eating? Is it nutritious? Or does it come in a box? According to the U.S government, a thrifty family of 4 spends $149.50 per week on groceries.

Low-cost vegan food is truly inexpensive. In other words, the external costs of processed food and animal products mentioned above do not apply when buying whole, plant-based, food. It is also entirely possible to purchase primarily organic produce on a budget as well if you spend wisely. I will show you how it is possible to adhere to the USDA's low-cost spending plan on a whole food, plant-based, vegan diet. Specifically, I will demonstrate and explain how an individual can spend $52 a week and still nourish her body with the best foods available.[4]

You may be questioning why I chose the second cheapest food plan, rather than the most modest spending plan. First, as noted, the USDA's spending plan is nationwide. It does not account for higher costs of food in Hawaii or expensive metropolitan areas like New York City or San Francisco. Therefore, the slightly more liberal spending plan is very thrifty in many portions of the United States. I happen to live in one of the more expensive metropolitan communities and know firsthand the price of food where I live far exceeds the cost of food elsewhere. Spending $38 a week is quite unrealistic in a place like Boston or New York City.

While food can be inexpensive and should be budgeted, there is a point where saving money and sacrificing quality has an adverse impact on health. Food and shelter are unarguably the two most essential components of our lives and budgets. Don't start thinking of food as a burden, or as an expense you invest little. Instead, I want you to think of food in terms of nutritional efficiency and cost-effectiveness. Food primarily needs to be good for the body. Then, you can focus on how much to spend on food.

The first chapter of this book goes over nutritional requirements and goals to be met, including vitamin, mineral and calorie intake for a moderately active adult female, 19-30 years old. I am using this demographic because the nutritional requirement for this woman is the commonly cited 2,000 calories per day diet. If you are a very active person or a man, 2,000 calories per day may not be enough for you.

The second chapter of this book focuses on general cost-cutting and cost-saving strategies.

The third and main portion of this book is a seven-day meal plan. The cost of each item is listed. Each day concludes with a breakdown of the food's nutrients, gross caloric intake, and the total cost. The chapter ends with a summary of the percentage of nutritional goals met over the course of seven days, total caloric intake, and total cost.

The fourth chapter wraps up with a reflection on the meal plan and total cost, tips for future budgeting, and suggestions for saving money on a vegan lifestyle.

Finally, the conclusion returns to the idea of the actual cost of food and explains why veganism is inexpensive and also has a low-impact on animals and the environment. In essence, the book concludes by reiterating how veganism is a truly thrifty and moral way to live one's life.

# Chapter 1: Meeting your Nutritional Goals on a Budget

To create a healthy vegan food budget, it is first necessary to define what a healthy meal plan is. This chapter will go over nutritional requirements for a moderately active female adult according to the United States Department of Agriculture's most recent Dietary Guidelines. These guidelines will be used later in this book to examine how meals made with a $52 budget fulfill ideal nutritional goals.

The USDA recommends that a moderately active adult woman (19-30 years old) consume between 2,000 to 2,200 calories per day. And, an older woman (30-50 years old) should consume between 1,800 to 2,000 calories per day. However, a calorie is not an accurate measure of your health or your food's nutrition. A calorie is a unit of measurement, like cups or miles, are. A calorie measures the amount of energy it takes to raise either one gram or one kilogram of water one degree Celsius.[5] We use calories to measure how much energy we burn. Calories have no insight into the quality of our food.

Using 2,000 calories as a base helps determine how much of each macronutrient (carbohydrates, proteins, fats) and micronutrient (vitamins, minerals) an adult female needs for optimal nutrition. In comparison, an elderly woman requires fewer calories than a moderately active adult woman. And, a younger man needs more calories than the 2,000 to 2,200 calories per day recommended for the women. Consult a dietitian or your family doctor for the appropriate daily calorie intake for you.

## *Macronutrients*

The USDA recommends a woman get 10-35% of her daily nutrients from protein.[6] However, studies have shown that high-protein diets above 20% contribute to some chronic conditions and even certain types of cancer.[7] Thus, I will aim for protein levels in the 10-15% range, based on advice from vegan nutrition experts like Dr. Thomas Campbell[8] and Dr. Douglas Graham.[9]

The USDA also recommends that 20-35% of an adult's daily nutrients come from fats.[10] However, it is essential to distinguish between the healthy fats that should make up this 20-35% and the unhealthy fats that should not be in your diet. The acids in fat are either:

- Polyunsaturated
- Monounsaturated
- Saturated
- Trans

We should strictly limit our consumption of saturated fat. Saturated fats are bad for you because they can raise your bad (LDL) cholesterol. High cholesterol often leads to heart disease and stroke.[11] Saturated fats are found primarily in animal products, so vegans are off to a great start.

Strictly limit, if not eliminate, trans fats in your diet because they raise the bad cholesterol and lower the good cholesterol (HDL).[12] Again, trans fats are found in animal products and processed snack foods.[13]

The fats we should be consuming are monounsaturated and polyunsaturated fats. These fats are essential for normal bodily functions, lower your bad cholesterol and can prevent heart disease and stroke.[14] Lucky for vegans, virtually all of our fat consumption comes in this form. Monounsaturated fats are in nuts, seeds, avocados, olives, and vegetable oils. Polyunsaturated fats can be found in vegetable oils as well.[15]

Carbohydrates in the form of fruits, vegetables, and whole, unprocessed grains should make up the bulk of your diet. The USDA recommends anywhere from 45-65% of your nutrients come from carbohydrates.[16] To reiterate, carbohydrates should come from whole foods and should be unrefined. Refined grains, found in processed foods, white bread, and crackers have gone through an unhealthy production process. During this process, these foods lose most of their vitamins and minerals. Processing diminishes important components, like dietary fiber, even the artificially-fortified, refined grains.[17]

In this book, I analyze the percentage of nutritional goals as a proportion of one's diet according to the USDA guidelines. However, for those at home, macronutrients are often displayed in grams on food labels, so I will provide you with gram conversions. Using grams allows you to figure out if you are meeting your macronutrient goals. To fall within the 10-35% protein range, someone on a 2,000 calorie diet should eat somewhere between 50-175 grams of protein. They should eat 44-78 grams of fat to fall within the 20-35% range. They should consume 225-325 grams of carbohydrates to fall within the 45-65% range.[18]

Let's examine micronutrients, vitamins and

minerals. The following is a list of commonly considered micronutrients and the amount required in grams on a 2,000 calorie diet. These recommended values come from The Mayo Clinic, the National Institutes of Health, and the USDA. Feel free to view my citations for more information regarding these recommendations.

- Fiber - 22-28 grams[19]
- Vitamin A - 700 micrograms[20]
- Vitamin B1 (Thiamine) - 1.1 milligrams[21]
- Vitamin B6 - 1.3 milligrams[22]
- Vitamin C - 90 milligrams[23]
- Vitamin E - 1.5 milligrams.[24]
- Calcium - 1,000 milligrams[25]
- Folate - 400 micrograms[26]
- Iron - 18 milligrams[27]
- Zinc - 8 milligrams[28]

There are plenty of other vitamins to examine. However, I have chosen to focus on these micronutrients because I believe they paint the best picture of a person's overall nutritional health as these vitamins and minerals come from an abundance of sources. If you are getting sufficient amounts of these specific nutrients, there is a very high chance you are getting enough nutritional intakes of other vitamins and minerals not included.

Now you have a general idea of what and how much of each macronutrient and micronutrient you should be getting on a 2,000 calorie diet. You may wonder how 8 milligrams of zinc and 50 grams of protein looks. Additionally, you may be curious how meeting all these goals can be accomplished on a tight budget. The good news is that optimal nutritional intake is both tasty and inexpensive! Now let's look at some cost-saving tips for a healthy lifestyle.

# Chapter 2: Veganism: An Affordable Lifestyle

Vegan and vegetarian diets tend to be cheaper than meat-eating diets because the cost of meat and animal products can be higher than many non-animal protein sources like legumes or tofu. However, a vegan diet can be expensive if you don't plan, budget, or be practical about where you purchase your groceries. For instance, you could buy expensive faux meats and frozen vegan products, or you shop at expensive boutique health food stores. Overall veganism costs what you want it to cost, and there are some ways to make it the most affordable lifestyle option.

First, vegan items can be bought at any grocery store, from the budget or bulk grocers to gourmet, top-of-the-line shops. Organic and vegan-friendly foods have become a substantial part of the food industry in the past decade. Therefore, most stores have a strong incentive to offer organic produce and healthier, vegan-friendly food options. I can purchase nearly everything I want at my local mid-range grocery store. Expensive health food stores are a rare occasion reserved for hard-to-find items or last minute preparations.

The price of food at farmer's markets and food co-ops vary drastically, so I am unable to say whether your local options would beat grocery store prices. However, food co-ops that offer pre-paid produce plans or purchasing food in bulk tend to be more cost-effective in the long run.

A pre-paid produce plan is an option where you pay in advance for a season and receive a weekly portion of fruits and vegetables at a discounted price. In general, buying food in bulk is an excellent way to save money because the unit cost tends to be much lower than if you bought it in standard form.

While purchasing organic food is always an outstanding choice for your body, it isn't always good for your wallet. There are some products that you can skimp on when buying organic to save a few dollars. These types of produce are called the "The Clean 15." The Clean 15 are:

1.  Onions
2.  Avocado
3.  Sweet corn
4.  Pineapples
5.  Mango

6. Sweet peas

7. Asparagus

8. Kiwi

9. Cabbage

10. Eggplant

11. Cantaloupe

12. Watermelon

13. Grapefruit

14. Sweet potatoes

15. Sweet onions[29]

One final way to save money is to make as many things homemade as you can, instead of buying the product in the store. For instance, you can make kale chips for $1.50 instead of buying them at the grocery store for $6.00-$8.00 per bag. Make your hummus with a 0.99¢ can of beans rather than buying pre-made hummus for $3.00. If you can make the nutritious food yourself, then you will save a lot of money.

# Chapter 3: The $52 Challenge

This grocery list is for a single person eating a 2,000 calorie diet. The list does not include spices, like salt, pepper, sauces, and cumin since I assume most people already have these items in their pantry. The prices reflect my local, mainstream grocery stores. So, these groceries may be more or less expensive in your area.

Without further ado, here is the grocery list:

| Item | Total Cost | Portion of Item Used (If applicable) | Cost of Portion of Item Used (If Applicable) |
|---|---|---|---|
| 18 Ounce Package Quaker Oatmeal | $1.99 | 9 ounces (1.5 ounce in a serving size) | $1 |
| Loaf of Whole Grain Bread | $4.50 | 12 Slices | $3.50 |
| 3 Bunches Bananas | $3.50 | N/A | N/A |
| 2 fifteen-ounce cans Garbanzo Beans | $1.50 | N/A | N/A |
| 2 fifteen-ounce cans Kidney beans | $1.50 | N/A | N/A |
| 2 fifteen-ounce cans Black Beans | $1.50 | N/A | N/A |
| 28 Ounce Organic Diced Tomatoes | $2.00 | N/A | N/A |
| 5 Medium-Sized Sweet Potatoes | $3.00 | N/A | N/A |
| 2 Apples of Choice (1 Pound) | $1.50 | N/A | N/A |
| 1 Navel Orange | $0.65 | N/A | N/A |
| 5 Ounce Package Organic Spinach | $2.50 | N/A | N/A |
| 5 Ounce Package Organic Kale | $2.50 | N/A | N/A |
| 1 Avocado | $1.25 | N/A | N/A |
| 2 Organic Roma Tomatoes | $1.50 | N/A | N/A |
| 16 Ounce Frozen Bag Sweet Corn | $0.99 | N/A | N/A |
| 50 Ounce Bag of Brown Rice | $4.99 | 18 Ounces | $1.08 |
| 1 Medium Pineapple | $2.99 | N/A | N/A |
| 16 Ounce Package Organic Strawberries | $2.50 (On Sale/Seasonal Fruit) | N/A | N/A |
| 64 Ounce Carton Plain, Unsweetened Almond Milk | $3.25 | N/A | N/a |
| 12 Ounce Bag of Chia Seeds | $6.29 | 4 Tablespoons | $1 |
| 14 Ounce Package of Extra-Firm Tofu | $2.25 | N/A | N/A |
| 1 Bunch Organic Broccoli | $2.50 | N/A | N/A |
| 1 Bunch Bok Choy | $1.29 | N/A | N/A |
| 13.66 Ounce Can Light Coconut Milk | $2.90 | N/A | |
| 1 Jar All-Natural, Organic Peanut Butter | $3.00 | 10 Tablespoons | $1 |
| 1 Yellow Onion | $0.90 | N/A | N/A |
| 1 Garlic Head | $0.40 | N/A | N/A |
| 6 Ounce Soy Yogurt | $0.90 | N/A | N/A |
| GRAND TOTAL | $51.35 | | |

You may be wondering how three meals a day and some snacks are going to come from this hodgepodge of ingredients. What exactly am I going to do with a bunch of bok choy and peanut butter you might ask? Hint: They are two separate meals. Anyone creative enough to combine bok choy and peanut butter, however, can be my guest!

# *Sunday*

**Breakfast**: Green Smoothie
- 3 Bananas
- 1 oz. Spinach
- 1/2 Almond Milk
- 1 tablespoon maple syrup, agave syrup, or date sugar if desired
- 1 Teaspoon Chia Seeds
- 1/2 cup sliced strawberries

1. Blend bananas, spinach, almond milk and syrup together.
2. Add chia seeds and sliced strawberries on top. Enjoy!

**Snack**: Peanut Butter on Toast
- 2 tablespoons peanut butter
- 2 slices toast

**Lunch**: Tofu Curry (Serves 4)
- 1 can light coconut milk
- 1 bunch bok choy
- 14 oz. package extra firm tofu
- 2 cloves garlic

- 1/2 onion, chopped
- 2 teaspoons cumin
- 1 teaspoon turmeric
- 1 teaspoon ginger
- 1 teaspoons chili powder/paste
- 2 cups uncooked brown rice (yields 4 cups)
- 1/2 tablespoon olive oil

1. First, dry out the tofu. Even though it is extra-firm, it will still have excess water in it that needs to be removed before you can properly cook it in a frying pan. To do so:
   a) Using a paper towel, press out any remaining juices.
   b) Then put a heavy object, like a book, on top of the tofu and let it sit there for about an hour. The book or other heavy object serves as a tofu press.
   c) Cut the tofu into small cubes.
   d) You can buy an official tofu press, but I find a book works just as well and saves money.
2. Chop up the onion finely and mince the garlic.
3. Wash and chop up bok choy. The bok choy can be in larger chunks. You can eat the

stem of the bok choy though I usually throw the whitest part of the stem away.

4. Place tablespoon of olive oil in a large frying pan and let the oil heat up on medium heat. Add the can of coconut milk, onions, garlic and spices.

5. Add the tofu to this mixture once it is boiling. Let the tofu cook for about 5-7 minutes. Then, add in the bok choy. Turn the heat to low and let it simmer for 5-10 more minutes.

6. Prepare the rice in a pot or a rice cooker. The general rule of thumb with rice is that you should add twice as much water as you have rice. For two cups of uncooked brown rice, you should use four cups of water. Cook until the rice absorbs the water. Brown rice takes longer to cook than white rice. It will take about 40-60 minutes.

7. Scoop one cup of cooked brown rice into a bowl. Pour a portion of the curry on top of the rice. I don't precisely measure out my servings. Eyeball it, reminding yourself you should be able to eat three more servings of the curry and rice.

**Snack**: 1 cup pineapple & 1 banana

**Dinner**: Mediterranean Sweet Potato
- One medium-sized sweet potato
- 1 cup raw spinach
- 1 Roma tomato, diced

For the Chickpeas (3 servings)
- 1 fifteen-ounce can garbanzo beans (chickpeas)
- 1 teaspoon cumin
- 1/2 teaspoon paprika
- 1 teaspoon turmeric
- 1 teaspoon garlic powder
- 1 tablespoon nutritional yeast (put on after cooking)

1. First, drain and rinse the chickpeas. In a strainer rub the skin off the chickpeas with a paper towel or your hands. The skin comes off easily, like a peel.
2. Sprinkle the spices onto the chickpeas and mix.
3. Place the chickpeas in the oven at 400°F for about 10 minutes.
4. Then, turn over and cook for about 5

minutes or so. The chickpeas should be crispy on the outside but not completely dried out

5.  You can either microwave the sweet potato or bake it. I think baked sweet potatoes taste much better, but microwaving it is much quicker.

    a)  To microwave, puncture holes into the potato and cook for about 5 minutes. Flip over halfway through.

    b)  To bake the potato, preheat the oven to 400°F. Make punctures in the potato and wrap in aluminum foil. It takes roughly 45-60 minutes to cook it. If you cut the sweet potato in half, however, that time is cut in half.

6.  Take your potato out of the oven. Place spinach, one diced Roma tomato, chickpeas, nutritional yeast and any dressings or spices already at your disposal. You may want tahini, nutritional yeast, or hummus.

Daily Totals

Nutritional Goals Met: 98%

Calories: 1934/2000

Protein: 12%

Fat: 25%

Carbohydrates: 62%

Fiber – MET

Vitamin A - MET

Vitamin B1 MET

Vitamin B6 – MET

Vitamin B12 – MET

Vitamin C – MET

Vitamin E MET

Calcium –MET

Folate – MET

Iron – MET

Zinc – MET

## *Monday*

**Breakfast**: Banana-Strawberry Oatmeal
- 2 bananas
- 1 cup oatmeal
- 1 cup almond milk and a little extra if necessary
- 1/2 cup strawberries

1. Cook two servings of oatmeal for about 2 minutes in the microwave.
2. Meanwhile, cut up bananas and strawberries into slivers. I like to warm them up with the oatmeal in the microwave, so it becomes more of a fruit compote, but that's up to you.
3. Sometimes, I'll sprinkle some flaxseed or chia seeds on top of the finished product as well.

**Snack**: Avocado on Toast
- 1/2 Avocado
- 2 slices of toast
- Salt and pepper to taste
- 1/2 of a medium-sized lemon, juiced

(optional)

**Lunch**: Tofu Curry

**Snack**: Fruit Salad
- 1 banana
- 1 cup strawberries
- 1/2 cup pineapples

1. Cut up the fruit into large chunks and mix in a bowl.

**Dinner**: Mediterranean Sweet Potatoes

Daily Totals
Nutritional Goals Met: 95%
Calories: 1982/2000
Protein: 12%
Fat: 25%
Carbohydrates: 63%
Fiber – MET
Vitamin A - MET
Vitamin B1 MET
Vitamin B6 – MET
Vitamin C – MET
Vitamin E – MET

Calcium - MET

Folate – MET

Iron – MET

Zinc – MET

## *Tuesday*

**Breakfast**: Chocolate, Peanut Butter, and Banana Smoothie
- 3 bananas, peeled and frozen
- 2 cup almond milk
- 1 tablespoon cocoa
- 1 tablespoon peanut butter

1. Blend all of the ingredients thoroughly.

**Snack**: Kale and Avocado Salad
- 2 oz. kale
- 1/2 avocado
- salt and pepper to taste
- 1 cup broccoli

1. Wash the kale and cut the leaves from the stems. The stems can be quite bitter and fibrous. Dispose the stems.
2. Place the kale in a large salad bowl. Make cross-stitch incisions in the half of an avocado. Scoop the avocado squares out onto the kale.
3. Either steam or microwave the broccoli

then add it to the dish.

4.  Chances are you may still need some spices like salt and pepper or a dressing to make this dish a bit more flavorful. Salsa would be an excellent, fat-free touch here.

**Lunch**: Tofu Curry (last serving, with extra half cup of brown rice)

**Dinner**: Mediterranean Sweet Potato

Daily Totals
Nutritional Goals Met: 97%
Calories: 1965/2000
Protein: 11%
Fat 27%
Carbohydrates: 62%
Fiber – MET
Vitamin A - MET
Vitamin B1 MET
Vitamin B6 – MET
Vitamin C – MET
Vitamin E – MET
Calcium - MET
Folate – MET
Iron – MET

Zinc – MET

## *Wednesday*

**Breakfast**: Strawberry-Banana Chia Seed Pudding
- 2 bananas
- 1/2 cup strawberries
- 1 tablespoon chia seeds
- 1 cup almond milk
- 1 tablespoon agave syrup or maple syrup

1. Place the chia seeds and the almond milk in a bowl and cover with plastic wrap. Leave the almond milk and chia seeds in the refrigerator overnight. When you take it out the next morning, the chia seeds and the milk will be congealed together, like a pudding.
2. Cut up the bananas and the strawberries into slivers. Place on top of the pudding. Drizzle the fruit and chia seed pudding with a sugar of your choice.

**Snack**: Banana

**Lunch**: Sweet Potato & Kale Buddha Bowl (Vegetable and rice salad)

- 1 medium sweet potato
- 2 cup broccoli
- 3 oz. kale
- 1 cup cooked rice
- 2 cups water (or vegetable stock)

1. To assemble the Buddha Bowl start with the brown rice base. The general rule of thumb is to use twice as much water as rice you plan on cooking. So, boil two cups of water.
2. Again, I prefer to bake my sweet potato if I have the time. However, microwaving the potato is also possible. To bake the oven should be at 400°F. It takes anywhere from 20-50 minutes depending on the size of the potato.
3. Wash the kale, remove the bitter stems and cut up the leaves. Dispose the stems.
4. Steam or lightly sauté the broccoli.
5. Add all the ingredients together and mix them in a large salad bowl.

**Snack**: Two Pieces of Toast with Peanut Butter
- 2 pieces of toast
- 2 tablespoons peanut butter

**Lunch**: Chock Full of Beans Chili

- 1 fifteen-ounce can dark red kidney beans
- 2 fifteen-ounce cans black beans
- 1 twenty-eight ounce can diced tomatoes
- salt and pepper
- 1 tablespoon cumin
- 1 tablespoon chili powder
- salt and pepper to taste
- 1 tablespoon olive oil
- 1 tablespoon cilantro
- 3 garlic cloves
- 8 oz. corn
- 1/2 onion
- 3 tablespoons tomato paste
- 2 cups water

1. Place 1 tablespoon of olive oil in a pot over medium-high heat. Add the chopped onions and crushed garlic. Cook the onions and garlic for about 5-7 minutes.
2. Then, add the water, tomato paste, and the large can of diced tomatoes.
3. Add the spices.
4. Let the spices and broth brew for at least 10-15 minutes before adding the beans and corn to the

mix.

5. Let everything simmer on low-medium heat for another 10 minutes or so before serving.

**Snack**: 1/2 cup pineapple

Daily Totals
Nutritional Goals Met: 93%
Calories: 1900/2000
Targets met: 93%
Protein: 13%
Fat: 23%
Carbohydrates: 64%
Fiber – MET
Vitamin A - MET
Vitamin B1 MET
Vitamin B6 – MET
Vitamin C – MET
Vitamin E – MET
Calcium – Almost (77%)
Folate – MET
Iron – MET
Zinc – MET

# *Wednesday*

**Breakfast**: Strawberry-Banana Chia Seed Pudding
- 2 bananas
- 1/2 cup strawberries
- 1 tablespoon chia seeds
- 1 cup almond milk
- 1 tablespoon agave syrup or maple syrup

3. Place the chia seeds and the almond milk in a bowl and cover with plastic wrap. Leave the almond milk and chia seeds in the refrigerator overnight. When you take it out the next morning, the chia seeds and the milk will be congealed together, like a pudding.
4. Cut up the bananas and the strawberries into slivers. Place on top of the pudding. Drizzle the fruit and chia seed pudding with a sugar of your choice.

**Snack**: Banana

**Lunch**: Sweet Potato & Kale Buddha Bowl (Vegetable and rice salad)

- 1 medium sweet potato
- 2 cup broccoli
- 3 oz kale
- 1 cup cooked rice
- 2 cups water (or vegetable stock)

6. To assemble the Buddha Bowl start with the brown rice base. The general rule of thumb is to use twice as much water as rice you plan on cooking. So, boil two cups of water.

7. Again, I prefer to bake my sweet potato if I have the time. However, microwaving the potato is also possible. To bake the oven should be at 400°F. It takes anywhere from 20-50 minutes depending on the size of the potato.

8. Wash the kale and cut it up so that the tasty leaves are separated from the bitter stems. Throw away the stems.

9. Steam or lightly sauté the broccoli.

10. Add all the ingredients together and mix them in a large salad bowl.

**Snack**: Two Pieces of Toast with Peanut Butter
- 2 pieces of toast

■   2 tablespoons peanut butter

**Lunch**: Chock Full of Beans Chili
- 1 fifteen-ounce can dark red kidney beans
- 2 fifteen-ounce cans black beans
- 1 twenty-eight ounce can diced tomatoes
- salt and pepper
- 1 tablespoon cumin
- 1 tablespoon chili powder
- salt and pepper to taste
- 1 tablespoon olive oil
- 1 tablespoon cilantro
- 3 garlic cloves
- 8 oz. corn
- 1/2 onion
- 3 tablespoons tomato paste
- 2 cups water

6.   Place 1 tablespoon of olive oil in a pot over medium-high heat. Add the chopped onions and crushed garlic. The olive oil should cook the onions and garlic in about 5-7 minutes.

7.   Then, add the water, tomato paste, and the large can of diced tomatoes.

8.   Add the spices.

9.   Let the spices and broth brew for at least 10-15

minutes before adding the beans and corn to the mix.

10. Let everything simmer on low-medium heat for another 10 minutes or so before serving.

**Snack**: 1/2 cup pineapple

Daily Totals

Nutritional Goals Met: 93%

Calories: 1900/2000

Targets met: 93%

Protein: 13%

Fat: 23%

Carbohydrates: 64%

Fiber – MET

Vitamin A - MET

Vitamin B1 MET

Vitamin B6 – MET

Vitamin C – MET

Vitamin E – MET

Calcium – Almost (77%)

Folate – MET

Iron – MET

Zinc – MET

## *Thursday*

**Breakfast**: Green Smoothie Bowl
- 1 cup almond milk
- 2 bananas
- 1/2 strawberries
- 1 tablespoon agave syrup (or date sugar, coconut sugar, or maple syrup. Refrain from white sugar).
- 1 tablespoon chia seeds

1. Combine spinach, almond milk, bananas, and sweetener in a blender. Blend until smooth. It will be a vibrant green.
2. Next to the berries, add the chia seeds. Sprinkle unsweetened coconut on top. You can drizzle Agave Syrup on top if you'd like.
3. Mix it all together, or enjoy all the ingredients separately.

**Snack**: 1 cup Pineapple

**Lunch**: Dill Chickpea Salad Sandwich with Kale Chips

For the Chickpea Salad Sandwich

- 1 fifteen-ounce can chickpeas
- 2 tablespoon Veganaise
- 2 slices toast
- 2 teaspoons dill
- 1/2 teaspoon cumin
- Salt and pepper
- 2 teaspoons Dijon mustard

1. Combine all of the chickpea filling ingredients in a food processor. You can also use a blender, but you will have to stop periodically to squash some of the chickpeas back down to the blade.

2. Process on low power. You don't want the chickpeas to become puree. The finished products should look more like chicken salad. In essence, the chickpeas should be broken up, and the spices and condiments should be evenly distributed. You should be able to see the chunks.

3. Place sliced tomatoes and lettuce on bread first and then scoop chickpea salad onto the bread. Give yourself a generous portion. Place the other piece of bread over the top

to make the full sandwich. Cut in half and enjoy!

For the Kale Chips
- 1 tablespoon olive oil
- 1 oz. kale
- 1 tablespoon Nutritional Yeast
- salt and pepper, to taste
- 1 tablespoon lemon juice

1. Remove the stems from the leaves then tear the leaves in half. The stems are quite fibrous and bitter. I don't like them when I use kale, in general, so I would suggest not including them in this recipe.
2. Toss the kale leaves with the olive oil, nutritional yeast, lemon juice and salt/pepper.
3. You do not want a thick layer of kale. A thick layer will lead to some being overcooked and some undercooked. Give the kale some space to breathe.
4. The trick to kale chips is to keep the baking temperature low. It takes longer to cook, but in the end it is worth it. Try 275°F, but 300°F may be okay depending on your

oven.

5. Bake for 10 minutes and then take out to rotate pan and shift the chips around a bit. Cook for another 10 minutes. In total, you should be baking them for about 20 minutes.

**Snack**: Apple with Peanut Butter and Almond Milk

- 1 apple
- 2 tablespoons peanut butter
- 1 cup almond milk

**Dinner**: Chili (Recipe explained above)

Daily Totals

Nutritional Goals Met: 91%

Total Calories: 2056/2000

Protein 14%

Fat 18%

Carbohydrates 58%

Fiber – MET

Vitamin A - 65%

Vitamin B1 - MET

Vitamin B6 – MET

Vitamin C – MET

Vitamin E – 70%

Calcium – 50%

Folate – MET

Iron – MET

Zinc – MET

# *Friday*

**Breakfast**: Chocolate Banana Oatmeal
- 2 bananas
- 1 cup oatmeal
- 1 cup water
- 2 tablespoons maple syrup
- 2 teaspoons cocoa powder

1. Cut up bananas into slivers.
2. Blend oatmeal and cocoa powder together before adding water to the oatmeal.
3. Cook in the microwave for 90-120 seconds.
4. Place the bananas on top of the oatmeal and drizzle the maple syrup on top.

**Snack**: 1 cup pineapple

**Lunch**: Chickpea Salad Sandwich

**Snack**: Apple with 1 tablespoon peanut butter

**Dinner**: Chili with sweet potato

Daily Totals

Nutritional Goals Met: 92%

Calories: 2019/2000

Protein: 13%

Fat 10%

Carbohydrates: 74%

Fiber - MET

Vitamin A - 65%

Vitamin B1 - MET

Vitamin B6 - MET

Vitamin C - MET

Vitamin E - 50%

Calcium - 40%

Folate - MET

Iron - MET

Zinc - MET

## *Saturday*

**Breakfast**: Vegan Banana Split
- 1 banana
- 1/2 cup strawberries
- 1 cup soy yogurt
- 1 tablespoon chia seeds
- 2 tablespoons maple syrup

1. Slice open one banana length-wise and place in a bowl.
2. Scoop out a generous amount of plain yogurt onto the banana. Roughly 1 cup or so.
3. Slice up about 1/2 cup of strawberries or the remaining supply for the week. Place on top of the yogurt.
4. Sprinkle chia seeds and drizzle maple syrup on top of the vegan banana split.

**Snack**: Orange

**Lunch**: Grilled Banana Peanut Butter Sandwich
- 3 tablespoons of all-natural, non-GMO, no sugar added, peanut butter

- 2 slices of toast
- 2 bananas, chopped
- Dollop of coconut oil or olive oil

1. Spread one and a half tablespoons of peanut butter onto each slice of bread.
2. Then, chop up your banana into medium-sized chunks, about 1/2 inch or less in height. Spread them evenly on both sides of the sandwich.
3. To grill my bread I usually use a toaster oven or my panini maker as it requires no oil.
4. However, if you do not have one of these items you can always grill it in a skillet. To do so, spread about one tablespoon worth of coconut oil in a pan over medium-high heat. Put the sandwich together and cook each side for about 3 minutes. A little bit of oil goes a long way and gives the bread that crispiness you don't get without the oil.

**Dinner**: Healthy Beans and Rice
- 1 fifteen-ounce can kidney beans
- 3 oz. corn
- 2 teaspoons cumin

- 1 clove garlic
- 1 teaspoon cilantro
- 1 teaspoon chili powder (optional)
- 2 cups cooked rice
- 2 tablespoons nutritional yeast
- 1/2 tablespoon olive oil

1. Bring 4 cups of water to a boil. Cook rice for 40-60 minutes until the water has been absorbed, but the rice is not completely dried out.
2. In a pan over medium-high heat, add 1/2 tablespoon olive oil. Mince garlic and cook in olive oil for a few minutes.
3. Drain and wash off beans. Put beans in a strainer. Add beans, corn, and spices (except the yeast and cilantro) to the pan and let simmer 5 minutes.
4. Remove pan from the stove top. Combine rice and beans. Mix thoroughly. Add cilantro and nutritional yeast to the meal.

Daily Totals
Nutritional Goals Met: 91%
Calories: 1998/2000
Protein 13%

Fat 18%

Carbohydrates 70%

Fiber - Met

Iron - 82%

Calcium - 78%

Fiber – MET

Vitamin A - MET

Vitamin B1 MET

Vitamin B6 – MET

Vitamin C – MET

Vitamin E – 40%

Calcium – 78%

Folate – MET

Iron –82%

Zinc – MET

## *Nutritional Summary*

First of all, I used the web software Cronometer to gather nutritional data for my meals. What goes into Cronometer's percentage of dietary goals data I include in this book covers far more macro- and micronutrients than I list each day. (i.e. it looks into Vitamin K, $B_{12}$, various types of proteins, etc.). The percentage set out in this book is based on Cronometer's detailed analysis. It is not just the portion of the macro- and micronutrients I have listed. I'm assuming most of you don't want to read 100 different micronutrients you are or are not getting for seven days straight. If you do wish to look at this data, take a look at Cronometer.

If anyone is concerned about their macro- and micronutrients, I highly suggest using Cronometer over other nutritional tools, which often just track calories or an insufficient number of vitamins and minerals. You use it by manually inputting the food and serving size of each meal or item you eat. Most often, someone has already submitted the food that you are trying to enter, and you can use their data for it. However, Cronometer allows you to enter new food items and information to its database as well.[30]

For the most accurate nutritional fit, please consult a licensed dietitian or your health care provider. Based on your specific nutritional needs, you may require more or less of any number of calories, nutrients, and minerals.

My goals for this week's eating plan were to:
1.  Meet at least 90% of my nutritional goals each day. One-hundred percent every single day is a great goal, but I can miss a few vitamins and minerals one day and make up for them in the next day.
2.  Fall within the healthy range of macronutrient proportions.
3.  Be within 100 calories of the 2000 calorie goal set at the beginning of this meal plan.

## *Summary of Weekly Nutritional Goals*

| Day of the Week | Protein % | Fat % | Carbohydrates % | Total Calories | Nutritional Goals Met |
|---|---|---|---|---|---|
| Sunday | 12% | 25% | 62% | 1934 | 98% |
| Monday | 12% | 25% | 63% | 1982 | 95% |
| Tuesday | 11% | 27% | 62% | 1965 | 97% |
| Wednesday | 13% | 23% | 64% | 1900 | 93% |
| Thursday | 15% | 18% | 58% | 2056 | 91% |
| Friday | 13% | 10% | 74% | 2019 | 92% |
| Saturday | 13% | 18% | 70% | 2001 | 91% |
| TOTAL AVERAGE | 12.7% | 20.85% | 64.7% | 1979.57 | 93.85% |

Let's recap the recommended numbers and proportions. What do these numbers mean? How did the 30-year-old female case study fare on her limited budget this week? She has done quite well since she met 93.85% of her nutritional goals. It is easy, tasty, and cost-effective to be a vegan.

The 12.7% protein proportion falls within the USDA's 10%-35% guidelines. Remember, the 35% is an excessive suggestion. Medical professionals don't even encourage bodybuilders to have this much protein in their diets. As noted above, high levels of protein can have adverse effects on health. Therefore, 13% protein is sufficient and still falls within the USDA's recommendations.

The proportion of 20.85% fat also falls within

the USDA's 20-35% guidelines. If you'll recall, the aim was to get as much unsaturated fat in the form of polyunsaturated and monounsaturated as possible. Saturated fats and trans fat, found in animal products and processed food should be strictly limited. This meal plan is on the lower end of the suggestion for fat intake and is primarily polyunsaturated and monounsaturated. The primary sources of fat came from:

- Olive oil
- Avocado
- Peanut Butter
- Chia Seeds
- Coconut Milk

The 64.7% of carbohydrates also falls within the USDA's 40-65% guidelines. Remember, since we are limiting the percentage of protein and fat, the percentage of carbohydrates increase which is precisely what a person needs in a healthy, vegan diet. Carbohydrates should be in the form of whole grains, fruit, and vegetables are and have always been staples of man's diet. What needs to be limited are refined grain products, bleached white flour, and processed grain-based desserts like crackers and cookies. Eating 250 calories worth of crackers or cookies is not going to be as healthy as consuming 250 calories of fruit or brown rice. While the carbohydrates in the meal plan are on the higher end, they are all good carbohydrates.

The goal was to consume 2,000 calories in a day. It would be irrational and obsessive to make sure this number is exact. The calorie needs are going to vary by how active you are on a given day. One tablespoon of olive oil varies a few calories depending on how exact you are, too. Essentially, life is too short to worry about 100 calories too few or too many. The outcome of 1,979 calories is incredibly precise.

Just a reminder: This female is moderately active, which means she walks about 2-3 miles per day and has a somewhat active day-to-day lifestyle. Perhaps she walks to work, takes care of children, or is at a job that doesn't necessitate sitting for 8 hours at a time. In my opinion, she isn't a coach potato nor an athlete. She's just an average person.

If you are sedentary or sit a lot, get some walking in or extra physical activity. If you are less active, then you may require fewer calories than the moderately active person. If you are a runner or an athlete, you may require more calories. This person should be able to sustain her weight on 2,000 calories unless she drastically increases or decreases her activity level. Finally, this is not a weight-loss or weight-gain diet. Please seek advice from your medical provider for what dietary needs that best suit your unique health conditions. Then, you can use some of these ideas to implement what will fit your health needs and spare your wallet.

# Chapter 4: Future Considerations

Hopefully, you found this meal plan interesting and appetizing. True, most of the ingredients are ordinary items like bananas, oatmeal, and brown rice. However, I hope some more uncommon ingredients like pineapple and avocado make up for some of the more mundane food items. Also, it's important having a well-stocked spice cabinet. The one time cost of these groceries may set you back a few dollars. However, spices last a long time, and they make a great addition to a bland bowl of rice and beans. Many spices have significant health benefits.[31]

Readers will note the distinct lack of processed or packaged foods in this meal plan. Processed food, especially snacks are economically ineffective. A frozen meal, vegan or not, costs $3.00 or so. If you cooked that meal at home, it would most likely be made with ingredients that cost a third of that and make multiple servings. The processed, and the pre-packaged food is marked up for the convenience of the item. Stray from buying pre-packaged hummus, guacamole, and frozen meals when you can quickly make these dishes at home.

You will notice there is also a lack of desserts. I am not against desserts and frequently have a small serving of non-dairy ice cream, dark chocolate, or homemade vegan baked goods. Indulging in a small 150-200 calorie dessert when you've eaten 2,000 calories of healthy, nutritionally dense food the rest of the day won't harm you. I just didn't include it in this weekly meal plan. Stockpile items like baking soda, baking powder, and chocolate chips are infrequent purchases used in baked goods. Though these ingredients that last awhile are inexpensive, the cost would skew the actual price of the meal plan if I were to include these items.

The meal plan in this book is for one person. In reality, many readers are buying food for their families or partners. If you handle buying food for your household, look at the USDA's spending plans that apply to you. Parents looking to cut costs should buy in bulk. Single-person households don't have the option to buy in bulk except in a few limited circumstances. For instance, it may be possible for a single person to buy things like beans and rice in bulk because they have very long shelf lives. Families, however, can save hundreds of dollars by belonging to a bulk food store like

Costco or from buying in bulk at their local retailer, co-op, or farmer's market. The money saved, by the way, usually comes down to the unit cost of each item. For instance, when you purchase a six-ounce box of rice, the unit cost per ounce of rice may be about 30 cents. When you buy a thirty-two ounce bag of rice, the unit cost is usually closer to 5 to 10 cents per ounce.

You may wonder how you can adhere to this $52 budget each week and not get bored. It is possible to have variety in your diet and save money at the same time. Admittedly, it would be rather depressing if you had to eat this same meal plan all the time. To keep this budget and not be bored, purchase cheap food in bulk and use a portion of your money on more uncommon items you love to eat.

Here are items to keep stocked, to help minimize costs and to allow yourself the pleasure of trying out new dishes:

- Brown rice, quinoa, farro, barley, and basically, any whole grain
- Potatoes - sweet, red, purple, etc.
- Bananas
- Oatmeal
- Beans - Save even more money by buying

them dried instead of a can

- Lentils
- Frozen bulk veggies and fruit - though they are not ideal, if you are a single person, this type of food can help cut down costs
- Peanut butter

# Conclusion

When we talk about the price of food, we also need to recognize the cost that food has on society, animals, and the earth. There will always be a price paid, such as water and land usage. We are not entitled to eat whatever we like without someone or something paying a price. Remember that the cost of food doesn't just affect our bank accounts.

When I sit down to a meal, I remind myself it is a blessing to eat so well. Buying food that harms the environment or any being means I am disrespecting the labor that went into this food and the planet's generosity. I am taking far more than I should without realizing the cost that extends beyond my wallet.

Veganism is not just inexpensive. It also puts the least amount of strain on people, animals, and the earth. The vegan lifestyle is eating so that every being has access to the planet's resources, and this is true, low-cost living.

# Thank You

Thank you for downloading my book and I hope you enjoyed it and found many things insightful. Furthermore, you can opt-in to my Book Notification Group to get all the latest information on free promotions, discounts, and future book releases. Go to http://eepurl.com/bfE46z to get signed up.

I would appreciate if you would take a minute to post a review on Amazon about this book. I check all my reviews and love to get feedback (this is the real reward for me - knowing that I'm helping others).

If you have any friends or family who may enjoy this book, please spread the love and gift it to them.

View my other work at Amazon Author Central.

# About the Author

Lewis Haas is a father of 3 girls and a freelance writer. He enjoys daily meditation, exercising and spending time with his family. Currently residing in Tampa, Florida, his favorite time of year is winter when he meditates in the great outdoors.

# Special Thanks

Emma Cogan for all of your input and hard work. Carol Langkamp for your administrative assistance, constructive criticism and help. Kelli Rae, for being an inspiration to everyone, whether vegan or vegetarian. Everyone at One Jacked Monkey, LLC.

# References

>Calcium. (2013, November 23). National Institute of Health: Office of Dietary Supplements. Retrieved from http://ods.od.nih.gov/factsheets/Calcium-HealthProfessional/

>Campbell, Thomas. 2006. *The China Study: Startling Implications into Diet, Weight Loss and Long-Term Health.* Dallas, Texas: Benbella Books.

>Dietary Guidelines for Americans. (2010) [PDF] United States Department of Agriculture Retrieved from http://www.cnpp.usda.gov/sites/default/files/dietary_guidelines_for_americans/PolicyDoc.pdf (2015, June 13).

>Folate. (2012, December 14). National Institute of Health: Office of Dietary Supplements. Retrieved from http://ods.od.nih.gov/factsheets/Folate-HealthProfessional/

>Graham, Douglas. (2006). *The 80/10/10 Diet.* Key Largo, Florida: FoodnSport Press.

>Healing Foods Pyramid. (n.d.) University of Michigan School of Medicine: Integrative Medicine.

Retrieved from
http://www.med.umich.edu/umim/food-pyramid/fat
s.html

>Healthy diet: Do you follow dietary guidelines?"
(2013, February 22). Mayo Clinic. Retrieved from
http://www.mayoclinic.org/healthy-lifestyle/nutritio
n-and-healthy-eating/in-depth/how-to-eat-healthy/a
rt-20046590

>Iron. (2015, February 19). National Institute of
Health: Office of Dietary Supplements. Retrieved
from
http://ods.od.nih.gov/factsheets/Iron-HealthProfessi
onal/

>Trans Fat is Double Trouble for your Heart Health.
(2015, June 19). The Mayo Clinic Staff. Retrieved
from
http://www.mayoclinic.org/diseases-conditions/high
-blood-cholesterol/in-depth/trans-fat/art-20046114

>Saturated Fats (n.d.) American Heart Association.
Retrieved from
http://www.heart.org/HEARTORG/GettingHealthy/
NutritionCenter/HealthyEating/Saturated-Fats_UC
M_301110_Article.jsp

>Seidenberg, Casey. (2014, January 7). "Spices and
their Health Benefits." The Washington Post.
Retrieved from

http://www.washingtonpost.com/lifestyle/wellness/
spices-and-their-health-benefits/2014/01/07/4f074f
24-6f2d-11e3-aecc-85cb037b7236_story.html
>Thiamine. (2015, January 5). National Institute of
Health: Office of Dietary Supplements. Retrieved
from
http://ods.od.nih.gov/factsheets/Thiamin-HealthPro
fessional/#h2
>The Truth About Fats: The Good, the Bad, and the
In-Between. (2015, February 3).: Harvard Health
Publications: Harvard Medical School. Retrieved
from
http://www.health.harvard.edu/staying-healthy/the-t
ruth-about-fats-bad-and-good
>Vitamin A (retinol). (2013, November 1). Mayo
Clinic. Retrieved from
http://www.mayoclinic.org/drugs-supplements/vita
min-a/dosing/hrb-20060201
>Vitamin B6. (2011, September 15). National
Institute of Health: Office of Dietary >Supplements.
Retrieved from
http://ods.od.nih.gov/factsheets/VitaminB6-HealthP
rofessional/
>Vitamin C (ascorbic acid). (2013, November 1).
Mayo Clinic. Retrieved from
http://www.mayoclinic.org/drugs-supplements/vita

min-c/dosing/hrb-20060322

>Vitamin E (2013, June 5). National Institute of Health: Office of Dietary Supplements. Retrieved from http://ods.od.nih.gov/factsheets/VitaminE-HealthProfessional/#h2

> What are Calories? What is a Calorie? (2014, September 26). *Medical News Today*. Retrieved from http://www.medicalnewstoday.com/articles/263028.php

>Zinc. (2013, June 5). National Institute of Health: Office of Dietary Supplements. Retrieved from http://ods.od.nih.gov/factsheets/Zinc-HealthProfessional/

---

[1] Jones, 2011. http://www.med.umich.edu/umim/food-pyramid/index.html

[2] Dean, 2014.

[3] United States Department of Agriculture, 2010

[4] $52 is an average taken from the USDA's $48.30 low-cost plan for females 19-50 and $55.70 low-cost plan for males 19-50.

[5] What are calories? What is a calorie?, 2014.

[6] Dietary Guidelines for American, 2010, p. 15.

[7] Campbell, 37.

[8] Campbell, 308.

9  Graham, 2006, p. 99.
10  Dietary Guidelines for Americans, 2010, p. 15
11  Saturated Fats, n.d.
12  The Mayo Clinic Staff, 2015.
13  Ibid, 2015, p. 24-25.
14  The Truth About Fats: The Good, the Bad, and the In-Between, 2015.
15  Healing Foods Pyramid, 2009.
16  Dietary Guidelines for Americans, 2010, p. 15.
17  Ibid, 29-30.
18  Healthy Diet: Do you follow dietary guidelines?, 2011.
19  Ibid
20  Vitamin A (retinol), 2013.
21  Thiamine, 2013
22  Vitamin B6, 2013.
23  Vitamin C (ascorbic acid), 2013.
24  Vitamin E, 2013.
25  Calcium, 2013.
26  Folate, 2013.
27  Iron, 2013.
28  Zinc, 2013.
29  Pau, 2010, May 13.
30  Cronometer, 2015.
31  Seidenberg, 2014.

28133275R00042

Printed in Great Britain
by Amazon